T0273762

Even the Hollow My Body Made Is Gone
by
Janice N. Harrington

Winner, 2006 A. Poulin, Jr. Poetry Prize
Selected by Elizabeth Spires

Even the Hollow My Body Made Is Gone

Poems by
Janice N. Harrington

Foreword by
Elizabeth Spires

A. POULIN, JR. NEW POETS OF AMERICA SERIES, NO. 29

BOA Editions, Ltd. ❦ Rochester, NY ❦ 2007

For information about permission to reuse any material from this book please contact The Permissions Company at www.permissionscompany.com or email permdude@eclipse.net

Publications and programs by BOA Editions, Ltd.—a not-for-profit corporation under section 501 (c) (3) of the United States Internal Revenue Code—are made possible with the assistance of grants from the Literature Program of the New York State Council on the Arts; the Literature Program of the National Endowment for the Arts; the County of Monroe, NY; the Lannan Foundation for support of the Lannan Translations Selection Series; the Sonia Raiziss Giop Charitable Foundation; the Mary S. Mulligan Charitable Trust; the Rochester Area Community Foundation; the Arts & Cultural Council for Greater Rochester; the Steeple-Jack Fund; the Elizabeth F. Cheney Foundation; Eastman Kodak Company; the Chesonis Family Foundation; the Ames-Amzalak Memorial Trust in memory of Henry Ames, Semon Amzalak and Dan Amzalak; and contributions from many individuals nationwide. See Colpohon on page 88 for special individual acknowledgments.

Cover Design: Geri McCormick
Cover Painting: "Evening Maples" by Richard Harrington, courtesy of the artist
Interior Design and Composition: Richard Foerster

BOA Logo: Mirko

Library of Congress Cataloging-in-Publication Data

Harrington, Janice N.
  Even the hollow my body made is gone / Janice N. Harrington. — 1st ed.
    p. cm. — (A. Poulin Jr. new poets of America series ; no. 29)
  ISBN 978–1–929918–89–8 (pbk. : alk. paper)
1. African American families—Poetry. 2. Southern States—Poetry. I. Title.

PS3608.A7817E94 2007
811'.6—dc22
                        2006030823

BOA Editions, Ltd.
Nora A. Jones, Executive Director/Publisher
Thom Ward, Editor/Production
Peter Conners, Editor/Marketing
A. Poulin, Jr., President (1938-1996)
250 North Goodman Street, Suite 306, Rochester, NY 14607
www.boaeditions.org

NATIONAL
ENDOWMENT
FOR THE ARTS

State of the Arts
NYSCA

CONTENTS

V

FOREWORD

Robert Lowell, musing on the poetic process, once said, "Memory is genius." A poet of memory himself, he must have known there is no possibility of authentic human identity, or wisdom, without memory. Memory, in tandem with our anticipation of the future, is what anchors us to the present and gives our lives meaning.

With the publication of *Even the Hollow My Body Made Is Gone*, Janice Harrington joins a long venerable line of poets consecrated to the act of remembering. Responding to a question about her guiding esthetic, she writes, "Family history, Southern rural culture, history, folklore, the labor that makes a life, and memory are veins of ore that run through the body of my work. But of all these, it is memory and the aspiration to musical language that most shape *Even the Hollow My Body Made Is Gone*."

Memory, and its embodiment in a colloquial, yet highly wrought musical language, are what originally drew me to Harrington's manuscript and what continues to pull me back into the poems and thrill me. We learn the story of Lillian and Webster and their children and grandchildren, a black family living a hardscrabble life in the rural South more than sixty years ago. Set on the cusp of the Civil Rights era, the poems chronicle a way of life that has long since vanished and follow the family on their eventual migration north, providing glimpses along the way of the changing times.

An early poem in the book, "Killed in Childbirth," presents the act of remembering in almost ritualistic terms. In it, a daughter brings her dead mother's clothes up from an earthen cellar where they are carefully packed away and tenderly launders them once a year. Like many of Harrington's poems, this is a poem not only about a specific memory, but, in a more general sense, about the process of remembering, recounting as it does the deep human desire to commemorate and be remembered. Harrington asks:

> Will anyone save the cloth-skin
> that once held your shape?
> Will anyone wash away its darkness?

In stepping out of the poem's dramatic situation to address the reader directly, Harrington enlarges the poem's scope and, in effect, accepts the task and sacred obligation of serving as memory's functionary.

As the book progresses, memory becomes an increasingly dominant motif, pulled apart and pondered from a variety of angles, as the poet searches for a definitive metaphor. In "Before a Screen Door" she writes:

> Memory
> has a fly's dumb enthusiasm, rubbing its antennae
> in blessing or ablution, dropping its sticky eggs
> into waste, circling back fiercely, fiercely
> trying to forget the touch of so many small deaths.

And, in "The Warning Comes Down":

> . . . memory is a mendicant
> shaking its palms, auguring these lives
> and their absolution.

And, in "Possum":

> In memory's midden this rubbish eater:
> sucker of yolk and entrails, the biter of mice
> coveting the blueing breads, bones, and maggotted meat.
> Our appetites are no bigger than we are.

For Harrington, memory and song are inextricably intertwined. In her "aspiration to musical language," her poems are no less than lyric, spiritual documents, sung stories that soar above the weight and repetition of daily life, transforming that dailiness into something rich and precious. Often the poet splices actual songs into the poems—nursery rhymes, chants, hymns, and popular lyrics—to evoke a particular era, a foot-tapping mood, a dreaming state of mind.

Joined together in the poem, memory and song unite the time-bound and timeless, the finite and infinite. Song is presented as circular and thus timeless, without end. The poet writes of lives like satellites, "held and bound by prescribed orbits," yet seems to know that within the finite limits of a life, or poem, the possibility to sing, to soar, to transcend our earthly limits, exists, as when she writes in "Turning":

Believe

> that you are a June bug tethered
> to a cotton string, ceaselessly turning
> but never enough, held by implacable delight,
> your blue-black wings flared and ringing.

Like a stringed instrument that continues to vibrate after the musician has ceased playing, Harrington's poems resonate. Without in any way simplifying or ignoring the darker side of life—pain, loss, death, injustice—Harrington is a celebratory poet who *sees* with the fresh, wondering eye of a child, but *knows* with the mind and heart of an adult. She knows, finally, that in the face of death, "only the song remains. Only ruminant memory / taking our lives in its tough mouth."

— Elizabeth Spires

To my beloved reader, R.D.P.

I

THE THIEF'S TABERNACLE

I am stealing the golden vessels of the Egyptians to build a tab-
ernacle to my God from them, far far away from the boundaries
of Egypt. If you forgive me, I shall rejoice; if you are enraged
with me, I shall bear it.

—Johannes Kepler

If I steal the wan light from these penitent clouds
and take from their pewter cups dull coins of rain,

if I plunder

> *Somewhere there's music*
> *How faint the tune*
> *Somewhere there's heaven*
> *How high the moon*

and lift the rifle-crack riffs
of calving icebergs, and pinch plastic wads
from the bellies of white-tailed deer,

if I purloin protons, all the negative numbers,
and seven of Cantor's infinities,

if the world's sweetness drips from my lips—
syrupy, nectareous, honey-wined cascades
of sweetness between full lips—

if I steal distance, the shifting sandhills, and every
syllable of Susquehanna, sultry, and solitude,

if I am stealthy and sly, and despite
securities, spider over the ledge to burgle

and leave you like the echo
of a man weeping in an abandoned house,

if I steal your gray-haired fear, the way
you wake each night to worry,

if I finger the last, morning-lit moment,
seconds before you swing
your legs to step into it—will you forgive me?

Faith is avarice.
Doubt covets.
I build a house for us. Rejoice.

II

WHAT THERE WAS

Pine, catalpa, pin oak, persimmon,
but not tree.

Hummingbird, hoot owl, martin, crow,
but not bird.

Cannas, honeysuckle, cockscomb, rose,
but not flower.

Wood smoke, corn, dust, outhouse,
but not stench.

A spider spinning in a rain barrel,
the silver dipper by the back porch,
tadpoles shimmying against a concrete bank,
but not silence.

A cotton row, a bucket lowered into a well,
a red dirt road, a winging crow,
but not distance.

A rooster crowing, cows lowing in the evening,
wasps humming beneath the eaves, hounds
baying, hot grease, but not music.

My mother running away at fifteen,
my grandmother lifting a truck to save a life,
an uncle at Pearl Harbor, Webster sitting
at the back of the bus when he looked as white
as they did, but not stories.

The entrails of a slaughtered sow, the child born
with a goat's face, the cousin laid on a railroad
track, the fire that burned it all, but not death.

This poem, a snuff tin sated with the hair
of all our dead, my mother's nighttime talks
with her dead father, my great-grandmother's
clothes passed down, passed down, but not memory.

KILLED IN CHILDBIRTH

Dust, stillness, the stench of raw earth,
each year, this same solemnity—
lifting the trapdoor to take the rungs
down and down into a room of sand
in search of a box that held nothing.

Nothing? A cardboard box tied by twine,
storage for two skirts, a cotton blouse,
a tea-colored slip, a lady's handkerchief
stitched with purple floss by hands
she had never touched, though she knew
the pockets their fingers had reached into,
and the hems they had raised and pushed aside.

Heirlooms washed and folded over a garden fence,
left for the sun to dry and the heat
to billow full again, as clothes will always
seek dimension. See—she was a short woman
and wide-hipped. She sewed. On Sundays
she wore a blue cotton blouse with velvet panels.
Her hems swished and smelled of red sand.
Nothing more. And the one who raised
the trapdoor and lifted the box asks, asks,
and asks, but they know nothing more.

Slip, skirts, blouse, hanky, she brings
them in, smooths the folds into fresh creases,
mummies each piece into sheet or pillow sham,
and restores them in a cardboard box
to sand, to darkness and cool unmoving air.
Will anyone save the cloth-skin
that once held your shape?
Will anyone wash away its darkness?

IF SHE HAD LIVED

If she had lived, the goat-faced girl,

she would have seen her reflection in the waters
of this fishpond and held its white-fleeced lilies
beneath her whiskered chin. If she had lived,

she would have walked in moonlight, pulling eel
from lampblack waters, while owls told their old spook
story, *Who'll cook for you? Who'll cook for you?*

If she had lived, she would have stooped
beneath the day's hem, back bent and arched,
chopping cotton as the minutes fell like hoe blades,
their sweated strokes sounding *thuh, thuh, thuh.*

Living, she would have proved that a colored woman
lay once with the Goat God, that a colored woman
held Faunus between her thighs and loved him.
Their fierce rut amidst yellow-eyed asters and red sand:

their kindled groins beside the nests of fire ants.
She lay beneath him and they loved, and they loved,
her flesh drinking the clabbered sperm.
This happened to a colored woman in Alabama,

and she gave birth to a goat-faced girl.
They say she had the breasts of a grown woman.
They say she was covered in hair. They say,
she had a goat's face: this child deformed.

The mother said the baby was born
with the face of fear, that ripe with this child,
she had seen a goat unexpectedly
and it frightened her, a goat and this warning:

that a woman must be careful, vision gives
birth to itself. The baby died, perhaps
it was born too old, perhaps a goat heart
is not strong enough. The baby died

and the mother buried her beside the garden,
or was it the fishpond? No, the baby is here,
in the Negro cemetery, her little fingers curled
inward, grasping. Later, the mother will cradle

her arms against her chest, her breasts spilling
milk. She will walk into the darkness remembering
her child, the goat-faced girl. The hooves of tears
mark her cheek, but she will not wipe them.

She stands in the dark, a colored woman, crooning,
crooning, crooning, and a wind comes: gentle.
A wind blows across her skin, across her lips, across
the ends of her fingers, making music—the sound of pipes.

In Alabama, a colored woman bore a deformed baby.
No, a colored woman bore the child
of a goat. No, a colored woman is grieving.
Her goat-faced girl, her baby is dead—that is the song, sing it.

Say, a colored woman is grieving her baby girl, sing it.
But this all happened long ago, the child is dead.
The woman is dead. They are gone, girl, woman, goat,
only the song remains. Only ruminant memory

taking our lives in its tough mouth.

SUPERSTITIONS THAT THE MULATTO PASSED ON TO HER DAUGHTER

I

Never step over a sleeping baby

Why was that?

If a child lies asleep on a rough-planked floor,
on a pallet, on red earth, do not step over,
shortening its life. Go around.

This is a black child. Do not step over.

In our footsteps, red dust,
the dust of place (Alabama,
cotton fields, a cast-iron bed,
the kitchen—where day begins
in a wood-burning stove, a dough
board, and a beating fist),
the dust of flour and smoke.

In our footsteps, red dirt
broken under a yella man's plow,
and his girl, yella like her daddy,
walking beside him as he turns
the rows. He'll grow cane,
or cotton, and the yellow-clayed sun
will drop its dusty light, and the heat
hang its traces upon their backs,
and the day will hallow its way to evening,
and a long walk home,
and a bath in a ten-gallon tub.

In these footsteps, all that we've carried,
the blackened skillets and mason jars,
the antimacassars and pillow shams,
the quilts, the feather ticks,
the crooked bones and good hair.

The footsteps of what we know,
that tobacco juice will cool a wasp's sting,
that you rub soap on a red bug's bite
and give your wounds to a dog to lick.

What falls on a child,
its mother's dust, the weight

of a dusty world, choking dust,
four colored girls on a church
pew shaking the dust
from patent leather shoes,
or a Greyhound bus beside
a red dirt road, dust
settling on empty seats.

The weight:
that she has believed
or not believed, the dust
inhaled.

2

Never leave your hair where others will find it

Lonely,
hair seeks entanglement.

Slattern,
it does not care where it lies.

Larcenous,
it will steal anything—dust, spells, smoke, odor, seeds.

Gluttonous,
it reaches and wears the world as a dangle.

The ebon-haired night
and its starry pins.

And my love's hair
silver and gray.

And my grandmother's snuff tin
filled with the hair of all our women:

        Pearl,

                Paralee,

                        Palestine.

These fine strings black and straight.
Our keepsakes.

3

Never eat fish with milk

At the supper table
these blessings:
corn bread, stewed tomatoes,
okra, possum patties, fried

corn, potlikker, fatback,
fried pies, buttermilk.

And these warnings:
mason jars with swollen lids,
bent cans, lockjaw,
mold, mayonnaise—left out,
hot sun, going bad—
scald your dishes, smell it first,

never eat fish with milk.

4

Never leave an ax or a broom in the house overnight

Because the broom will beat you.
Because the ax will chop you
and a wise woman always knows her assailants.

Because of the banal misogyny
of all we've constructed,
can you trust a plate?
Is the rug lying in wait?
At night, each thing admits its nature.
When you're naked and alone, or not
alone, roll over, extend your hand
into the emptiness. Wait.
In the kitchen, something will move,
a hem of straw, and then a blade's footfall.

HENRY OSSAWA TANNER'S "THE BANJO LESSON," 1893

How does it feel to run the tip of one
finger along the edge of a banjo wire?
Which is heavier, a banjo
or an old man's breath?

The sound of banjo strings
plucked by a colored boy is the sound
of twanging, of *tur-pen-tine, pine tar, plank,*
of pennies of rain spattered on scalded tin.

Boy and man frailed by light and strokes
of paint, surrounded by chair, table, kettle,
crock, a cooling skillet, a pipe exhaling
smoke, and mystery: beside an unseen
pane—a black coat: journey, the small
griefs we throw across our shoulders.

Between daylight and firelight,
these bright embers, O trembling
strings! Darkness is never satisfied.
Beside the useful plates, pitcher, and bread,
on the table's altar cloth, these questions:

Should we buzzard lope and knee bone bend
in a ring dance of stuttered steps, or strike
the drumhead, strum, strum, strumming
strident chords? Should we pluck the reeling
notes or embrace and blow embers into flame?

Pull a vein from your right ventricle,
stretch it taut, slant one thumbnail and pluck it.
Listen—does it sound anything like rain?

BEFORE A SCREEN DOOR

Over a darkening spill, water lilies tip,
tadpoles beat against a concrete bank,
and all the banty hens take to their beds
beneath catalpa limbs. Evening comes,
weary evening, and Webster sighs skeins
of clothy smoke, beginning his accustomed
meditation: a wooden match and *Prince Albert.*
Crimp cut. Long burning pipe and cigarette tobacco,
the moments rolled, twisted, and licked with a dull tongue,
while—*swap swap!*—before him, perched
on a weathered edge, his grandchild holds
a fly swatter's stem and plastic slapper,
convinced—*swap swap!*—that she can kill
them all, bluebottle, horsefly, housefly,
flesh fly—all the incessant buzzers.
Quietly, Webster tells her to stop,
then smokes and watches, powerless
before insatiable conviction. Smoke
and splintered wings, these offerings to a distant God,
and in each plastic slap, in each rasping sigh—a psalm.

Skillet,
        muscadine,
                kerosene,

molasses—years later, beside a back door: blowflies,
spring maggots rising from cedar mulch and rot.
I do not wonder whose death has brought them,
or ponder the blossoming flesh, but if they hold
a message, if they whisper *Mercy, O mercy,*
their voices are no stronger than the pleading multitudes.

Skillet,

      muscadine,

            kerosene—yella-burning

in a black night, molasses—these things will attract
flies, sweet things, even death. Believe the body
is a screen door. Believe that peering from behind
the screen is this sign, a little girl in a red dress
and bare feet, a colored girl standing stork-legged
in a red dress. And the fly that bump-bumps
against the screen is also a sign, perhaps corruption
or hunger, a conviction, loss, anything
you can't shoo or kill enough. A fly's wings
are translucent cellophane, divided
like the heart or the tablets of the commandments,
two blades, two tongues, abuzz, abuzz,

Diptera,

      bluebottle,

           blowfly,

housefly, flesh—a child sits before
her grandfather, killing flies. Memory
has a fly's dumb enthusiasm, rubbing its antennae
in blessing or ablution, dropping its sticky eggs
into waste, circling back fiercely, fiercely
trying to forget the touch of so many small deaths.

BURNING THE RAIN FOREST

I watched Webster hold an ax blade to a gray
stone spun round and round, its sharp scry
and steel-gray skin shedding chips of light.

A Fourth of July sparkler in a child's hand
is a silver dandelion. And in the evening,
I watched Webster, after a long day

in the fields, return home in overalls
to sit on the front step or porch to smoke.
He rolled a papery skin, yella as his own,

a thin sheath tap-tapped with crumbled leaves
from Prince Albert's tin. And there beside
the front porch step, beside his long legs,

he showed me the number of 9s hidden
on Prince Albert's red tin: see there,
and there. . . . And then he struck a match

with a saffron thumbnail, amber and hard
as iron, stunning a sulfury spark. On the back
porch, before supper, Webster taught me not

to waste—to wash my hands in a basin
of well water, taking only a palm of its gray
shade, only the smallest drops. This hard

lesson: one I wouldn't learn, wanting
it all and everything in copious amounts.
Given the choice I would save nothing,

would spill, squander, waste, lavish
for delicious joy: well water shiver-spilling
on red sand. And I waited patiently, once,

as he tried to twist my ropes of hair
into braids but made plows and traces, made
the shredded leaves of his smoking tobacco,

made fishing line held taut in a bullhead's
mouth, made wood smoke and the urgent bay
of a red-boned hound—the things he knew.

Standing over me, inept at this one thing:
his grandbaby's hair. Webster tall
and flaming with red hair like the burning

bush or a kerosene lamp, like the pine logs
on a winter fire, the fire we stared into,
he with his pipe and me wide-eyed staring

and not blinking into the flames until tears
came and pipe smoke rose like an offering
to some faraway god. Follow the smoke, follow

the man or follow the girl, and they
will come here: a small basement room
and a gift from my grandfather, a dollar bill

with his initials "WP," and a house on fire,
burning, destroying everything we own but not
this: my payment from a man of fire, this story,

out of ashes, out of smoke, the currency of memory
writ small on a burning leaf, all we love afire, held
close to the heart's steel, these splintered sparks.

In Mexico the rain forest is burning,
and its smoke drifts over Illinois.

In Mexico the rain forest is burning,
and child, I can see the smoke from Illinois.

HEAT

And the mornings were cast iron.
The men's overalls, the women's hair,

and the nights were cast iron. The clatter
of kudzu leaves was the clatter of iron lids.

And the flies that settled wore cast-iron wings.
And the stench of the outhouse was a cast

iron stench, and the baby's cry fell heavy
as a frying pan. And the rain was cast iron,

each splat of gray a skillet lid, each spill
a kettle of potlikker. Their beds were cast

iron and so too the thighs wrapped round
his hips and the way he shook and withered

out. The heat was cast iron, and the greasy
sun dripped its lard light against their skin,

sweat welling like water sprizzled on a hot
griddle. And their skin was cast iron,

and living was fatback, turned slowly
and browned, what you had to eat, even

if it wasn't the best. And cast iron their sleep,
cast iron their throats and their jubilee.

If a man is paid eight cents for a pound
of cotton that is cast iron too. If he leaves

for Detroit or Kansas City or Chicago, he'll pack
a cast-iron suitcase and fill it with cast iron.

And if he says, *Things'll be bedda up there,*
his smile will be seasoned and impermeable.

REVIVAL

Through the cooling dark,
they walk, Lillian, Webster, Riley, Anna,
MacArthur and Eurel, returning
from *Heavenly Father* and *Yes, Jesus!*,
from paper fans with little brown
girls in Sunday bonnets—*M-hmmmm*—
from the communion of sour juice and crackers,
ah weh-lll, from church mothers in nurses'
uniforms and rills of sweat spilling from black brows.
Have mercy on us, Father.
Look down upon us, Father, and give us
your blessing, in Jesus' name . . .

Above a darkened bough, a wing
beats, and in the pitchy shadows crickets
shrill, and a frog repeats, repeats,
repeats. Maybe Anna holds her father's
hand. Maybe the boys tussle and pitch
stones into darkness while their mother
watches, humming and holding
her Bible more firmly than an ax handle,
or maybe they go weary on and quiet.
It is only their steps you hear, only shifting sand.

On a rural route, a family walks
while the night begins its long sermon,
and the miles go by, and the miles go by.
If an owl calls from that darkness,
then someone will die. If a hound keens
one long, longing vowel, they will shudder.
If a star plummets, that too will have meaning.
This is faith, the road that takes them home.

DRYING APPLES

Kneeling, she leans onto one hand
and with the other pushes apple slices
and rings of apple, spreading them
wide across flattened flour sacks
beneath the heat and desiccant air.

Even sweetness is labored for, even
this moment disturbed only by distant
sawing, only by a crow's desolation,
and by her hand moving out, around
and out again, unsettling the morning hour.

Earlier, she snapped wennish apples
from their stems and dropped them
into a bushel basket. She washed them
with well water, throwing aside the ones
that floated, the ones too wormy. She sat
in a straight-backed chair beneath a pin oak
with paring knife and five-gallon tub,
curling away the blotchy peel, stabbing
seeds and woody stem, cutting away
the spoil and all that was not pap or apple.

Now, unworried, she presses a papery sliver
against her tongue, holding its wedge
between brown lips—an epistle
that life is reach and bend, is arm, is leg,
is back, is imperfect, is rot and worm,
is too small, is not enough; it is bitten,
it is chewed and sucked, it is swallowed
or spat out, and it is sweet, it is sweet, it is sweet.

Now she spreads apples atop a shed
she built herself, atop its slanted roof,
spreading and smoothing pats of appley
flesh that will wither and dry, wither
and brown. She will shuffle the pulpy
ruffles into cotton sacks, reduced
and earlike, ears filling both palms,
relics of a martyred saint or the wizened
tongues of castrati singing *hush hush hush,*

but . . . no, they are only apples,
only dried apples in a flour sack
light and easy to carry, a bounty set aside,
preserved for need or long winter
or an appetite that craves splendor—
not its shape but its remembrance.

CORN CRIB

Follow the road past fire pit and catalpa,
past the tires semicircled on end.
Step, gently, over the barbed wire's border,
over the pasture's hoof-beaten sand,
over its hills of fire ants and saw-edged grasses,
and you will find settled there like a half-buried
bucket or a work-wearied man, a school bus,
the one they used to carry colored kids
from biscuit to book and back again,
its sides weathered and yellow,
the windows latched by dust,
Lamar County Training School
writ clear as letters in a basal reader.

Pushed, the door divides like a saltine.
The driver's seat sits erect and shoulders back.
Driverless, it can't be accused or asked *why*
or *how long* or *when* but waits like a juror's chair
before the sightless windshield. In the silence:
the echo of tires on a rutted road,
the whine of a school bus suddenly
stopped, the bird-singing of children,
and lunch pails bang, bang, banging
against metal rails. Gears, steering, brake,
the wounded gash that held the keys,
mirrors rear and side, the radio tuned
to wasp and crow and the hum of flies,
and down the long aisle on either side,
over the rectangled seats, under
their thick green slabs and sprung coils, spilling
along aisle and floor: a corn flood.
Yellow corn on red-and-white cobs smelling
of chickens, and the chicken-shit stink

of chicken yards, and rain-wet chickens
with inky feathers and reptilian feet.

Still it is not the smell that suffocates
but the cast-iron heat, not the chickeny stench
but the burdened air, the dust of dust and corn dust,
the dust of cracked kernels and desiccated silk,
the drifts of unsweepable dust. And the corn standing
waist high and higher sprawls yellow, yellow,
yellow. And the falling sun slants through silted
windows, kindling the motes until everything is molten
and motion, and the corn feels like bones in your hands,
bicuspids and molars mortared to a rough rod.
The corn feels like a burning brand
or a baton held up for unknown victory.

In a year, the roadsides of Anniston will wait,
broken teeth plucked from bloodied mouths,
mobs hundreds strong. Passengers beaten.
Metal pipes beating, beating, and buses set afire.
Then other buses set afire, and other fires.
The world burns in so many places.
Black smoke rising, rising.

You lift an ear of corn, twisting the kernels
until they burst free, and for a moment,
you think this must be hope: small,
brittle-hard, and plain as this, a searless flame,
a fodder set aside in a yellow school bus.
But in the next moment, you know that it is not.
Turning again to take the steps, you feel the kernels
beneath your heel, a yellow grist filled with dust
and ground by every step into grit and cooling ash.

TURNING

In the side yard, this small hub: a child
clasping a cotton string bound to a June bug's legs.

Maybe the iridescent minstrel will weary and die.
Maybe its leg will shear and cast off its bridle.
Unfortunate machine, maybe it doesn't know
we are held and bound by prescribed orbits.
Yet the child will never weary,

not of a June bug's hums, the way it strums the air
like a sawmill in the distance or the low murmur,
m-hmm, of a Baptist Church on Sunday morning,
nor will she tire of its turning. How many times
around? Never enough. Turn

and you are that cotton string, a well's rope,
an unraveling doily, or the yellow thread
that cinched Webster's tobacco pouch. Turn
and you are a June bug's dolorous drone.

Traveler, believe the stars are bright beetles
tied to strings of light. Believe that a brown girl wields
these lambent arcs, that wild vibrations
tremble the tips of a brown girl's fingers. Believe

that you are a June bug tethered
to a cotton string, ceaselessly turning
but never enough, held by implacable delight,
your blue-black wings flared and ringing.

III

THEY ALL SANG

I

Even the cast-iron skillet sang
of grease, and heat, and bloodied meat,
summoned the reaching flame,
gladsome despite its heavy skin.

Even the well bucket rang like a Baptist choir
or a man toppling down a stair who laughs,
denying the frailty that his child has witnessed.

They all sang: the saw, the hound,
the clamoring crow, the cow's shofar,
the tooth against the dipper's rim,
the whetstone, and the kudzu's hem.

Only the persimmons did not sing,
choosing instead to cinch pressing
lips and draw them tight with discontent.
But the bed sang, with the body's
oar and chantey, its springs singing:

> *Jordan is wide, boys, Jordan is wide.*
> *Heave away, Jordan, heave away.*
> *Find no rest 'til the other side,*
> *Heave away, Jordan, heave away.*

And the screen door above the back step sang,
why when going in and *why* when going out,
though no one answered.

And the wasps above the outhouse stench
sang angrily, angrily, all day long, all day long.

2

Hands washed in a pan of well water sing
of soil and soap and splash and splintery light,
sing abundance and probity,
sing of palms and bodies embracing
in the darkness of a cast-iron bed.

And the hands sodden with well water
are the hands that will raise a pine switch
to whip a child: *which! which! which!*
Listen, beloved, listen—in each nick, a note
of blood and a child singing, *oh,* and *oh.*

3

Beneath the eaves of loblolly and yella pine
children sing *Little Sally Walker,*
sittin' in a saucer. Rise, Sally, rise.
Wipe your weepin' eyes. Put your hands
on your hips. Let your backbone slip . . .

and *London Bridge is falling down,*
falling down, falling down. . . .

Children who know before their sixth year
four synonyms for sorrow—cry, weep,
bawl, and all gone, baby, all gone—
sway and shimmy, standing
on bright earth, dark dancers:

O shake it to the East.
O shake it to the West. Shake it
to the very one that you love the best!

Children who know the falling
down of things and know the hands
that lock you in and knock you
back and forth, zeal's violent theatre,
they know the tightened fists and linked limbs
that hold us imprisoned between two towers
and chant in the stunning light, *falling
down, falling down.* Falling

down, two brown-legged girls in cotton dresses,
girl-towers, brow facing brow,
hands raised in an arch above their heads,
sunlight in sooty hair, terrible fire:
they will be the towers
beneath an inconceivable sky,
their arms falling, falling.

Rusty-knees and ashy elbows,
children singing, singing,
until one of them is chosen.
Take the key and lock her up!
Lock her up! Lock her up!
Take the key and lock her up,
my fair lady.

And you know they are not singing of death,
        my fair lady,

or towers falling,
        my fair lady,

or brutality's warders,
        my fair lady,

but of vast loveliness,
        my fair lady,

brought for safekeeping into these small hands,
into the spanning arms that make the human cradle,
O my fair lady.

WAITING

Beside the front porch,
there was a peach tree,
and on the porch,
in front of the peach tree, a swing,
and on the swing a girl.

The girl was small
with long legs. She sat upside
down, legs up, head down, swinging
back   and forth.

Beside
the swing, but along the porch,
was a rail
and in the rail a hole,
and down the hole a tunnel,
and in the tunnel a wasp,
a wasp that sealed itself in
with mud, with mud,
with mud, with mud,
and died.

The girl was swinging
back   and forth, back
and forth.

The swing
had a broad bench
held by metal chains,
and *E-rrrrr, AH, EE rrrrr-*
ah, Errrr-ah was the sound
of its swinging.

ASH

Vernon, Alabama, 1961

I think about that winter in Vernon
when it was just the two of us and cold,

and December sifted snow over the red
dough boards of yard and roof,

and you made the terrible pilgrimage each night
in bare feet from bed to stove, to stoke its embers

and add the meager coal. Afterwards, you shivered
across the linoleum, across its worn and cinder-

bitten roses. Do I remember you leaping
from petal to petal, your sallow feet shining

like beacons? I don't know. It was long
ago. But I know you climbed beneath

the sheets and—opening your shirt—
placed my hands against your belly.

We lay banked beside each other, unmoving,
asleep in a house as slanted as a cant of snow,

where we were *Websta's gal and her baby girl*,
where we waited for the colored serviceman

who belonged to us, until waiting
was also winter, a weather we knew.

How lovely we were then, the two of us,
huddled in that darkness, surrounded

by the dull glowing of red roses
and comet-cinders, cast out and briefly bright.

FALLING

With lengths of string and canted chairs, my father
struggles to raise the wide wings and bright belly,
every attempt unraveling, breaking, or crashing.
On crooked knee he tries again, but it never flies.
In the ancient story, another father watches
as his beloved plunges into the sea, leaving
only these signs: wax and twine and the quills of gulls.
But what father ever binds the cords tight enough?
Shy from that scalding sea! Shy from that searing
light! Aspire less and take the midmost course,
the one your father chose. Lift yourself on wings
he made for you, and when you fall into the devouring
sea whisper *Daddy, Daddy, oh,* but loud enough
for him to hear, loud enough to soften wax or sever

a gull's extended wing. In a backyard, in Vernon,
a colored man attempts to teach his daughter *flight*
and *boundlessness,* their shadows stretching
wingtip to wingtip, while between them
an airplane teeters on a cotton string but never
flies. And black Icarus plummets into a Tuskegee
airfield, a black bird from a clear sky,
a crow's field holler when you are the only one
to hear it. Dark Icarus riven against
red sand, black Icarus swinging, swinging
from a yella pine. The black feather that falls
upon your shoulder weighs more than grief.

No, the plane never flew. But we forgive
our fathers their broken flights: sometimes.
Aileron, airfoil, wing root, wingtip, we lift
ourselves through perilous moments unaware,
beneath pinions of mercy. How are wings

made? Wax, twine, and the quills of gulls?
And in the ancient story, a fisherman,
a plowman, and a tenant farmer from Sulligent
look up in amazement, seeing father and daughter

walking across the clouds. It is evening now,
and the heart has done its barrel-rolls
and loop-the-loops, and whatever we've written
on this pale page turns to vapor and rains
down into the sea. There is only this last act: rising,
full throttle into a breathless fall.

THE WARNING COMES DOWN

I

A colored woman stands beside a red dirt road
watching these strangers, these gypsies.
And hadn't her eye twitched just that morning,
nerve-whipping like a wire. This sign:
a jumping eye and company coming.

They offer to augur the future, to repair
the broken. They ask for well water,
but she gives them nothing, runs them off.
Not like Webster, who would have given
them anything, even the heart out of his chest.
With her, family would always come first.

But later she'll discover her missing trove:
all that she saved, tied in a handkerchief
and hidden in a steamer trunk, gone.
She will blame the gypsies for her grief,
the warning will come down.

An object lesson, you see how people do?
You learn that trust cannot be given,
never tied tight enough, or its loss shriven.
How two eyes in the back of your head
are too few. And people will steal the hinges
from the gates of hell, if you let them.

2

When my father came home, on leave,
he brought us a mason jar filled

with francs, centimes, and sous
and taught me to say *s'il vous plaît, bonjour,*
parlez-vous français, and hold a cup
with my pinky up as gentle ladies do.

A mason jar of French coins, that is absence.
Loss is the sound of it shaking, how we
were marooned, mother and daughter,
without him, to red dirt, to cleaning
other people's houses, poke salad,
and knowing we were poor but clean.

And now the chanson of centimes and sous
lies buried beneath red soil, resounding
in a colored child's coppered skin
and the whisper of spilling sand.

France is where daddies go,
overseas, in silver-bellied planes, and maybe
they'll come home again, tomorrow, tomorrow.

But now the days, minutes, months are all AWOL,
flat as francs, *un, deux, trois, quatre, cinq.*

3

And maybe this is 1960,
and I'm a colored serviceman
waving goodbye to a wife and child.

Or maybe I'm the daughter,
copper-eyed, searching desperately
for shoes, on bare feet calling, *Bye! bye!*
Bye, bye, Daddy!

Maybe I am a mason jar.

No, I am the father, a colored
man in khaki, leaving
in a yellow station wagon
and a hem of red dust,

going back to France or Germany,
to an Air Force base, to the other
who will lean his body into mine,

his longing a ripe persimmon,
sweet, swollen, and my mouth made
round swallows the black seed,
the orange flesh, and centimes

fall from my mouth, and red sand,
red, sperm-sand spills everywhere.

4

And the past, the handkerchief
of a colored woman, unties itself.

And in its cotton corners
all the missing, all we've tried to save.

And memory is a mendicant
shaking its palms, auguring these lives
and their absolution.

Beneath the Eiffel Tower
a Romany child pinches the moon between two fingers,
its tambourine light ringing against a hard world,

and the darkness swirls like a gypsy's skirt.

5

What is the half-life of a copper coin?

What grows from a buried jar of centimes and sous?

From the economy of our losses?

In Vernon, at the Old Negro Cemetery
amid scrub grass and red sand
this grave, the sky-blue tombstone

of a colored woman who went to Nebraska
and Kansas, once, but never to Paris,

beneath the pine-splintered shadows, the graves of many,
each a buried coin, under the turpentine heat
and the wind's green needles, whispering,
s'il vous plaît, s'il vous plaît.

THE OFFER

On cinder blocks beside a concrete bank,
Anna poses ladylike and ankles under,
her red-sirened lips parted slightly,
her forehead tilted to one side—a sable-eyed
starlet, circa 1955.

Only a polka dot shift hides her fullness.
How many months? Maybe four, maybe five,
or perhaps this is the last month.

And in the pond at her feet: waterlilies.
Waterlilies for the *yella gal*,
while over her shoulders lean pin oak,
persimmons, and cords of kudzu.

If a fish sounded from those green waters,
a fairy-tale fish tendering a life beneath
the black-bordered wet of her daddy's pond,
she would not have gone, contented then.

Only her belly stirred. Only the soft,
guppy-mouthed pulp pushed for a moment
at those warm bounds, reaching
for this brief chance and aquifers
secret, secure, and far away.

O BELIEVER

Bridal veil, lilies, catnip, rose—
beneath a pin oak tree a yella woman
rakes leaves and bracken as a snake unpeels
itself, slow, unwinding down above her head,
and the yella woman feels that long black reaching
and runs screaming, *Snake! Snake!*

And the colored children come, curious,
and her own brown babies watch
as a big boy comes to shoot it with his rifle,
missing and missing and missing until
finally the snake drops, hanging
for a moment like a question, a tongue
about to speak and deciding: not.

Some liquid part of the tree unwound,
each leaf made serpent, reptilian bark coiling
into roots. He takes it away, the big boy, takes the snake
to a ditch, or maybe he goes with it from house
to house to show: the snake that scared the yella woman.

O believer, Sistah Eve
wasn't tempted by no snake—but by that tree,
a tree showing its true nature: wanting,
and wanting God's attention to itself.
It was the tree that tempted her and not the snake.

The snake hung suspended over
a yella woman's head, over her yolk-skin, wanting
only to swallow her, or to lie against her skin, warm.

And her brown babies stand on one leg,
scratching behind one knee with the other foot,

watching their mama and this danger. Only
her oldest will remember, will hold the molted
skin of this memory: a snake molasses-winding
from a pin oak tree, understanding about temptation
and longing, how it is dark and sweet, how it hangs
over us, quietly watching, drawing closer.

POSSUM

I

A child points
                outside,
beside a rusted cypress:
this scuttling.

They squat together, child and woman
peering into the darkness, under
a rind of light, seeing

a screwed face and bad dentistry,
a jagged pelt aglow, its dirty tallow
burning just outside their window.

It snarls at them,

at these two shadows peering, one
delighted by fear, and one
amazed.

Is this how the past approaches?

2

I see them,
growling and raising their long
claws

in the razored light,
these dogs.

But I don't do what they suppose, fall
down, faint, overcome by possibility,
by fear, by habit,

or pretend that tooth, claw, and an imperfect
sense of mystery are the only defenses.

No, I turn my nose to them,
show them my teeth, fierce snarling
to let them know: I am a poet!

3

Fifteen baby possums will fit in the bowl
of a teaspoon.

4

From the compost
        rinds and rottings,

from the garbage
        peels,

from the shadows' darkness, darkness,
        this guttered meal and all its redolence.

What we were, what we were shaped to be,
fasts on waste.

What we are points its vulpine head and sniffs
but the next minute has no scent, and the minute
before is already carrion: eat.

In memory's midden this rubbish eater:
sucker of yolk and entrails, the biter of mice
coveting the blueing breads, bones, and maggotted meat.
Our appetites are no bigger than we are.

From the compost
       rinds and rottings,

from the garbage
       peels,

from the shadows' darkness, darkness,
       this guttered meal and all its redolence.

Why do you dine on refuse and avoid the banquet?

5

Possums are immune to rattlesnake venom.

6

And the possum has mastered these lessons:

of persimmons—
time and energy vibrating on a string of light
equals sweetness;

of night—
in the absence of color all things reveal
themselves by shape, smell, or trembling;

of prehensile tails—
look down! The world is uncertain.

We shake like Quakers above a molten fire,
small embers spinning on a ball of fire;
swaying back and forth, on our prehensile tails,
signal lights before an impossible engine;

of playing possum—
this is faith: arise and walk!

of jacklighting—
stunned we hold ourselves still
on a dark branch, death?

Or a lover's touch just there—ah! Still.

7

Infant possums inside their mother's pouch,
inhaling the same air, suffocate.

8

The hounds bay
and Webster's voice bawls
through the piney woods. Trembling,
the kudzu turns green ears
to the distance: listen.

The mind runs, climbs,
scuttles, leaps, scramble-stumbles
and burrows into briared dream.

Hiding for one brief moment before
the rending, the night's belly torn
open, its blasted heart pounding

ca choom, ca choom, ca choom, blood spilling
its red sand, its red sand, its red sand, spilling

for one brief moment.

Fireflies blink under a stand of pine,
an owl calls *hu hu, hu-huuuuu,*
hu hu, hu-huuuuu.

On its dark branch, the jacklighted
moon glints at a stunned world,

and a possum scurries away.

9

In Vernon,
a colored child is given a possum patty
for breakfast, a patty sweet with salt
and red-peppered. She holds greasy fingers
up to her grandmother. *Meat, Big Mama,*
meat! and is given another.

In Vernon, a colored child is given
a possum patty from a heat-smoky skillet,
and it is salt-sweet, greasy, and generously
peppered, large enough to fill both her hands.

THE LINE IS SLACK

I know tonight what I've always known,
remembering when she walked beside his long
swing of legs before dawn, before the cast iron
clatter or the rooster's stuttered roll,
the two of them together in the darkness,

and how she told it—
muslin mists rising from the cotton rows,
the moon a lye-washed sheet,
and from the boughs of pine and pin oak
the owl's lonely mourn, *wu whu, wu whu.*
The two of them, these best beloved,
father and daughter, walking hand in hand,

her daddy a tall, yella man
gleaming in the moonlight, with weathered
hat and tar-trimmed fingers,
wearing overalls and good strong boots,
carrying bucket and lantern, waking her,
to go with him down to the bottom
to check the lines and lift the nets.

In the chilling dark through barnyard,
under barbed wire, past the huge pasture gate
and the lullaby of cows, over a log bridge,
they walk together, lantern held high
beside the river bank, musky damp
and the night's psalm: bullfrogs, mosquitoes,
water giggled by the fins of fish, and bump,
bump, bump against a log the breathless
heaving of catfish trying to escape.

She watches her daddy's big hands
pull and pulling, raising the poles, reeling
the line and the night's bounty, maybe lamp
eels writhing like snakes, maybe luminous
bellied catfish, perch, turtle or frogs dead
and dangled. Afterwards, beside the bank,
her father's silence, the two of them sitting
in the blue-black quiet, waiting. Dawn
flares at last like the end of a cigarette.

Maybe she looks at him, her daddy, and knows
that she loves him, that what he raises
from dark water is not fish or eel but some
heavy part of the future, when he is not there.
At the end of a long line, her heart beats
and hangs like dangled bait, held out to the eternal,
to the darkness, to these heavy waters, knowing
that something will reach for her, that she'll be consumed.

TRAVELER

October 4, 1957. Soviets launch the first artificial satellite.

I

Every 98 minutes
the past tries its voice.

Its telemeter
measures the distance.

Memory: a satellite

numinous

and small
as a basketball.

2

This is when they left Vernon, heading North in a yellow station wagon. Anna in the front seat beside Charles, staring out at the plum-black night, gazing at its immeasurable pricklings, a night as wide as the River Jordan, wide, wide, and far above.

And the oldest child, awake, looks up into that vastness and thinks—as a child can—this world is beautiful, this black sky is beautiful, these sleepers are beautiful, and I am safe.

A Negro family going North, one of thousands leaving Tupelo, Montgomery, Valdosta, Chattanooga, Lynchburg. Against the black night the drumming of tires, in a tire's percussion the sound of loss. A night lingering like the smell of fried chicken. And from a sleeping fist the spill of corn-bready stars, yellow, white, and ashy gray.

The dashboard lights reflect against black glass. Dark woods, dark fields, and dark towns go by unattended. Charles rests his hand steady on the wheel. Anna stares into the darkness. The road repeats *swing low, swing low, swing low*. Another car passes by. Other travelers passing by, going somewhere they heard was better.

3

This is how it ends,
and the hens at rest on catalpa limbs
sheltered their heads under rusty wings and slept.

This is how it begins.
They went into the yard then, all of them,
when Riley came home saying
that something was following him,
something in the sky, a blackness.

Lillian went out, peering
beneath arched fingers. All of us went out,
every face raised, searching
for signs, for an omen or meaning.

We stood beside the chicken coop,
beside the smokehouse, waiting,
looking up and out into distance,
suspended between the fatbacked
and the unseen. Lillian stared skyward.

While above them, five hundred miles
in the darkness, in the gelid stillness,
a distant attendant, *small*, they say,
as a basketball, pilgrim dancer, dizzy-

spins its star-cast shadow, and reflected
on its metal skin: Andromeda, dust-spewed
gaseous nebulae, radiant novas, meteors,
tail-lashed comets, vibrating strings of light,
solar winds buffeting the arc of the universe,

O starry night!

Maybe what followed Riley
was only the impossibility of this moment.
Maybe what followed was a warning, a sign,
a portent, or the ablating orbit of a man's life,
perhaps yours, though Lillian never knew,
could not decide, and everyone went in again,

unanswered. The twilight bruised itself
to black, and the hens at rest
on catalpa limbs sheltered their heads
under rusty wings and slept.

V

A COLORED WOMAN CANNOT SING

of metallic hydrogen, amethyst
or anemone, turtle shells beside
an empty bed, or broken diadems.

A colored woman cannot sing
of Hasidim, the salt-rimed stones of Antioch,
how the Aegean tastes of sperm, and a sturgeon
squeezes black garnets from its rectum.

A colored woman cannot sing of I-beams
or derailleurs, the impact of microwaves
on Southern dialect, Froebel blocks,
or the smell of milk on your mother's nipple.

A colored woman cannot sing of tangerine
juice spilling on the ankle of a white girl,
tangerine mist on a white ankle. A colored

woman cannot sing of standing stones,
why dark matter in the galactic halo must
be nonbaryonic, or even hum "The Marseillaise."

A colored woman cannot sing
of pilgrims casting garlands into the Ganges,
one hundred red spiders dancing on a gray web,
or Nanjing and seven heads bobbing in a greasy pool.

A colored woman cannot sing
of minuets and manatees, the flutter of moths
on an infant's tongue, nutmegs and *milagros*,
or black tulips buried in a field of snow.

BENHAM'S DISK

is a toy with patterns of black and white. When it spins, the eye sees arcs of color.

I Mutation

Beside a rolling tire, a child skips,
striking its side, *a-tap, a-tap*, with a green switch.

Over 90 percent of the matter
in the universe is invisible.

On the phone, her niece exclaims,
Yesterday I was white but now I'm black.

Purple flowers are symbols of mourning
in Ixmiquilpan.

In the next moment, a chromatophore's
mutation may alter everything.

Evolution: mottled moths on a gray chimney.

In China, white is the color of mourning.
The moonlight weeps.

Six blind men cannot see an elephant.

Roll a pomegranate against a hard surface.
Perforate the skin: suck.
Garnets of juice roll down your chin. Let them.

Mulatto: *of mixed breed, from the Spanish for mule.*
Anything that cannot reproduce itself.

Vision is born of violence. All your memories
are mulattos.

In Mammoth Cave, a woman opens her hand.
Inside her palm—more darkness.

Evolution: a child born the color of mourning.

2 About Light

Italicized words express early Renaissance ideas, adapted from
Alison Cole, Eyewitness Art: Color.

To make a purple dye, crush Purpura
patula snails in a black cauldron.

Maggots floating in yellow broth.

For brown paint, seventeenth-century artists
ground Egyptian mummies to powder.
Tomorrow, grind a memory to dust.
Compare its color to an old lampshade's.

Wear a white rose if your mother is dead.

In sixth grade, Sister Amata said
that without light, there is no color;
everything is black.

Bright and clear colors reflect
the beauty of God's creation.

Her father never let her wear red.

Mixed colors, being corrupted,
are inappropriate for expressions of divinity.

Light: what we each absorb, what we reflect.

In Pippin's *Man on a Bench*,
a man rests easy on a red bench,
his arm angled and draped against red slats,
his foot stretched out and crooked,
just a man restin' easy on a red bench.
No one sits beside him.

Her father said only niggers wear red.

3 Chromatophore

A pigment cell, esp. one capable of changes of form or concentration
of pigment, causing changes of color in the skin.

Beside an abandoned mine,
rhubarb stalks push through black dust.

With slaked lime and vinegar,
        I could paint your skin.
With burnt bone and chimney soot,
        I could paint a woman weeping.

Open
your eyes! Open
your eyes! Open both eyes!

My hand rests against the ridge of my husband's hip.
A brown hand, dark knuckled, it lies there exposed.

I love you. Why camouflage tenderness?

My niece calls and exclaims, *Guess what.*
Yesterday I was white but now I'm black.

Let a red bench stand for a man's life.
Sit him upon it, throw his arm back against its red slats,
sprawl his legs outward. Squint a little and look.
See? A body caught in barbed wire. A body on the edge
of no man's land and the wire is red, red, red.

Salt, tenderness, heat, and insubstantial light:
the skin's vocabulary.

4 Color Blinded

Hydrangeas require acidic soil to change color.

In Urbana, a woman throws her wardrobe away.
The chart says her season is winter;
pastels are inappropriate.

A jump rope with green handles and a long-legged girl.
Say, a jumpin' rope and a long-legged girl.

Bumblebees see hues and patterns
invisible to the human eye.

Chromatic: *1. Of or pertaining to color or colors.*
2. in music, utilizing freely the half-step
interpolations in the diatonic scale.

In a Jewish cemetery, a man tosses a trowel of sand.
A scale of notes slides from each grain, grief's descant:
yellow sand falling into an open grave. The man weeps.

Tomorrow, without race,
we will go like blind men searching for elephants.

Say we're all jumpin' rope with that long-legged gal.
Say we're all twirling a green-handled rope, waitin' a turn
with that long-legged gal.

The insufficiency of vision: what haven't you seen?

A blind man holds an elephant's trunk, crying aloud:
We have reached paradise. O Eden's black serpent!

SHAKING THE GRASS

Evening, and all my ghosts come back to me
like red banty hens to catalpa limbs
and chicken-wired hutches, clucking, clucking,
and falling, at last, into their head-under-wing sleep.

I think about the field of grass I lay in once,
between Omaha and Lincoln. It was summer, I think.
The air smelled green, and wands of windy green, a-sway,
a-sway, swayed over me. I lay on green sod
like a prairie snake letting the sun warm me.

What does a girl think about alone
in a field of grass, beneath a sky as bright
as an Easter dress, beneath a green wind?

Maybe I have not shaken the grass.
All is vanity.

Maybe I never rose from that green field.
All is vanity.

Maybe I did no more than swallow deep, deep breaths
and spill them out into story: all is vanity.

Maybe I listened to the wind sighing and shivered,
spinning, awhirl amidst the bluestem
and green lashes: O my beloved! O my beloved!

I lay in a field of grass once, and then went on.
Even the hollow my body made is gone.

NOTES

The Thief's Tabernacle: "Somewhere there's music. . . . How high the moon": from "How High the Moon," 1940, lyrics by Nancy Hamilton and music by Morgan Lewis, a jazz standard and a signature song for Ella Fitzgerald.

They All Sang: "Little Sally Walker. . . .": words from a traditional African-American children's ring game.

ACKNOWLEDGMENTS

I am grateful to the editors of the journals where some of these poems previously appeared, sometimes in earlier versions.

Beloit Poetry Journal: "Benham's Disk," "The Line Is Slack," "Superstitions That the Mulatto Passed on to Her Daughter";
Field: "A Colored Woman Cannot Sing," "Corn Crib," "Henry Ossawa Tanner's 'The Banjo Lesson,' 1893," "What There Was";
Harvard Review: "They All Sang";
Indiana Review: "Heat";
Marlboro Review: "The Warning Comes Down";
Ninth Letter: "The Offer," "The Thief's Tabernacle," "Traveler";
Phoebe: A Journal of Literature and Art: "If She Had Lived";
Prairie Schooner: "Possum";
Seattle Review: "O Believer";
Seneca Review: "Falling";
Southern Review: "Before a Screen Door," "Burning the Rain Forest";
Tar River Poetry: "Ash."

I am grateful for the support this work received through an Illinois Arts Council Artists Fellowship Award in Poetry. I am also grateful to the editors of the journals that published poems I was not able to fit into this book, and especially to the editors of the *African American Review*, the first journal to accept my work.

ABOUT THE AUTHOR

Janice N. Harrington's poems have appeared in many journals. She is also the author of two children's books, *Going North* (Farrar, Straus & Giroux, 2004) and *The Chicken Chasing Queen of Lamar County* (Farrar, Straus & Giroux, 2007), and winner of many awards including the Ezra Jack Keats Award from the New York Public Library. After growing up in Alabama and Nebraska, she now lives in Champaign, Illinois, where she is a librarian at the Champaign Public Library.

BOA Editions, Ltd.
THE A. POULIN, JR. NEW POETS OF AMERICA SERIES

COLOPHON

Even the Hollow My Body Made Is Gone, poems by Janice N. Harrington, with a Foreword by Elizabeth Spires, is set in Centaur, a digitalized version of the font designed for Monotype by Bruce Rogers in 1928. The italic, based on drawings by Frederic Warde, is an interpretation of the work of the sixteenth-century printer and calligrapher Ludovico degli Arrighi, after whom it is named.

The publication of this book is made possible, in part, by the special support of the following individuals:

Anonymous (5)

Craig Challender • Susan DeWitt Davie

Dale T. Davis & Michael Starenko

Peter & Sue Durant

Jacquie & Andy Germanow

Kip & Deb Hale

Patti Hall & Joseph Shields

Tom Hansen

Robin & Peter Hursh

Archie & Pat Kutz

Nora A. Jones, in memory of Max N. Rogers

Craig & Susan Larson

Catherine Lewis & Angela Bonazinga

Stanley D. McKenzie

Marianne & David Oliveiri

Richard Peek • Boo Poulin

Steven D. Russell & Phyllis Rifkin-Russell

Joseph Turri • Ellen Wallack

Thomas R. Ward, in memory of Jane Buell Ward

Michael Waters

Dan & Nan Westervelt

Mike & Pat Wilder

Glenn & Helen William

www.ingramcontent.com/pod-product-compliance
Lightning Source LLC
Jackson TN
JSHW081320130125
77033JS00011B/375